My First Book about the African Animal Alphabet

Amazing Animal Books
Children's Picture Books

By Molly Davidson

Mendon Cottage Books

JD-Biz Publishing

Read More Amazing Animal Books

Purchase at Amazon.com

Download Free Books!
http://MendonCottageBooks.com

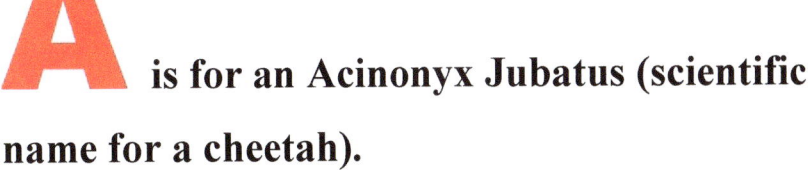 **is for an Acinonyx Jubatus (scientific name for a cheetah).**

Cheetahs are the fastest land animals; they can run up to 75 miles per hour (mph).

Their claws do not retract (pull in) so they cannot climb tall trees.

 **is for a Baboon.**

A group of baboons is called a troop.

Baboons are loud, hairy monkeys; they have hair everywhere expect their muzzles and a patch on their bums, used for sitting.

C is for a Camel.

A camel's hump stores a fatty tissue, which they can use for energy.

Camels have three layers of eyelids to help protect them from the blowing sand.

D is for a Desert Warthog.

Desert warthogs live in groups called "sounders;" they are usually just women and babies, the men like to live alone.

Warthogs dig burrows to live in; they usually enter backside first, so they can defend themselves from an attack with their tusks.

E is for an Elephant.

The elephant is the heaviest animal on land.

It weighs up to 6 tons (12,000 pounds), that is almost the weight of a school bus!

Baby elephants live inside their mothers for 22 months (almost 2 years!) before they are born.

 **is for a Fennec Fox.**

A fennec fox is the smallest of all foxes.

Its big ears help it hear insects and rodents hiding underground.

G is for a Giraffe.

A giraffe is the tallest land animal, they stand between 14 - 18 feet.

Giraffes will sometimes fight with their necks; this is called "necking."

Babies are born being 6 feet tall, and they grow an inch per day, for the first year.

 **is for a Hippopotamus.**

Hippos are cousins to the whale; this is why they weigh so much, about 3,300 pound.

The word hippopotamus is means "river horse" in Greek.

They live in rivers, swamps, and lakes; and eat mostly water plants.

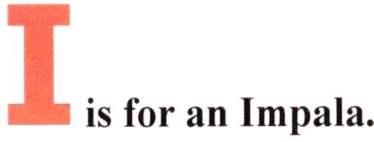 **is for an Impala.**

An impala is an African antelope, and there are plenty of them.

Only the boys grow horns, which they use to battle for girls and for their territory.

They are only about 3 feet tall.

 **is for a Jackal.**

Jackals are relatives of wolves, and are the most active early in the morning or late at night.

They scavenge for food, as well as hunt small animals.

 **is for an African Pygmy Kingfisher.**

Steve Garvie © <u>Wikimedia Commons</u>

The African pygmy kingfisher's main food source is spiders, but they also eat frogs, grasshoppers, worms, praying mantis, dragonflies, and cockroaches.

It is one of the smallest types of kingfisher birds; it is about 5 inches long.

L is for a Lion.

A lion's roar can be heard as far as 5 miles away.

The girls do most of the hunting; they hunt at night, and most of the time in groups.

Lions spend about 20 hours a day just resting in the shade.

M is for a Mongoose.

A mongoose is a relative of the meerkat.

There is always one mongoose on the lookout for predators, especially big birds; they are in charge of sending a warning cry to everyone else.

They eat insects, small birds, and rodents.

 is for a Nile Crocodile.

The Nile crocodile only lives in rivers, swamps, and marshlands in Africa.

The Nile crocodile is one of the most dangerous crocodiles; they kill hundreds of humans every year.

They rest in the hot sun with their jaws open, it helps keep them cool.

O

is for an Orycteropus Afer (Scientific name for an Aardvark).

MontageMan © <u>Wikimedia Commons</u>

Aardvarks are also called the African ant bear, because they eat mainly ants.

To escape predators they can burrow in the ground very quickly or they run in a zig zag pattern.

P is for a Patas Monkey.

Alex Roberts © <u>Wikimedia Commons</u>

Patas Monkeys live on the ground, mostly n the open savannas and deserts of Africa.

Their tails can reach a length of almost 2 1/2 feet.

Patas are the fastest monkeys running almost 35 mph.

 **is for a Rhinoceros.**

Rhinos mark their territory by rubbing their foot in their dung, then walking, creating a stinky barrier.

Rhinos can eat up to 110 pounds of food, which is mostly plants and trees, in one day.

Rhinos spread mud on themselves to stay cool.

 **is for a Sable Bull.**

Sable bulls are a type of antelope, they can stand as tall as 4 1/2 feet and their horns can be as long as 3 1/2 feet.

When boy sable bulls fight they fall to their knees and just use their horns.

T is for a Topi.

Topi are one of the fastest antelope; they can run up to 44 mph.

The Maasai people say the Topi looks like it is wearing jeans and yellow boots.

Both boy and girl topi defend their herds territory.

U is for a Ugandan Kob.

The Ugandan kob is another type of antelope; they live in the Saharan Desert.

The Ugandan kob is on the Uganda coat of arms.

They are a reddish brown color which is different from other kobs.

 **is for a Vervet Monkey.**

Purves, M. © <u>Wikimedia Commons</u>

Vervet monkeys live in the African forests; eating fruit, flowers, seeds, spiders, grubs, and locusts.

 **is for a Wildebeest.**

The wildebeest, also called a gnu, is a relative of the bull, and the largest game animal in Africa.

Baby wildebeests weigh about 46 pounds at birth, and can walk within minutes of being born.

Wildebeests travel in herds of about 150.

 **is for a Water Buffalo.**

(Yes, two W's because we skipped Q, did you notice?)

Alexander Vasenin © <u>Wikimedia Commons</u>

They spend much of their time submerged in deep water.

Water buffalo eat mostly plants, and live in large herds.

 **is for Xenus.**

Hans Hillewaert © <u>Wikimedia Commons</u>

Xenus are a ground squirrel that lives in South Africa.

They only weigh 1 to 2 pounds.

 **is for a Yellow-Billed Stork.**

Derek Keats © <u>Wikimedia Commons</u>

They have a black tail, which shines with colors of green and purple.

The yellow-billed stork lives in Africa and Madagascar.

Z is for a Zebra.

The zebra is cousins with donkeys and horses.

Zebras have stripes that help camouflage them in the tall grasses where they live.

Every zebra has their own stripe pattern; no two zebras are the same.

Download Free Books!

http://MendonCottageBooks.com

Our books are available at

1. Amazon.com

2. Barnes and Noble

3. Itunes

4. Kobo

5. Smashwords

6. Google Play Books

Download Free Books!
http://MendonCottageBooks.com

Publisher

JD-Biz Corp

P O Box 374

Mendon, Utah 84325

http://www.jd-biz.com/

Mendon Cottage Books

P O Box 374, Mendon Utah 84325